Contents

Cracow: Cultural Heart of Poland

Cracow was once the heart of a medieval Polish empire stretching from the Baltic to the Black Sea. Many Polish cities were badly damaged in the Second World War (1939-1945), but the walled city of Cracow, with its medieval streets, churches and palaces, is still full of reminders of its ancient past. It is seen by many Poles as the cultural capital of Poland.

In 1989 over forty years of communist rule in Poland came to an end (you can find out more about this on pages 6–7). This led to great changes. During the communist period most people in Cracow were employed in state-run industries, such as the Nowa Huta steelworks, and they lived in municipal flats. Luxuries were scarce but necessities were cheap and nobody had to worry about finding work. During the 1990s a lot of people lost their jobs as many of the state-run factories closed.

Cracow is now home to many new businesses. Today, jobs in private businesses outnumber those in state industries by almost ten to one. The queues and rationing of the 1980s are gone and the new supermarkets in Cracow are full of goods. However, adjusting to the changes that are taking place is still a challenge for many of the people who live there.

▲ Young Poles enjoy a lively youth culture amid the historic surroundings of Cracow's medieval centre.

◀ This Cloth Hall in the middle of the main square of Rynek Glowny dates back to the 14th century, although it was rebuilt in the 16th century after a fire. Inside, dozens of craft stalls sell craftwork and upstairs is the National Gallery of Cracow.

THE CHANGING FACE OF
POLAND

Text by CHARLES AND BARBARA EVERETT
Photography by JENNY MATTHEWS

WAYLAND

Produced for Hodder Wayland by
White-Thomson Publishing Ltd
2/3 St Andrew's Place
Lewes BN7 1UP

Editor: Alison Cooper
Designer: Christopher Halls at Mind's Eye Design, Lewes
Proofreader: Philippa Smith
Additional picture research: Shelley Noronha, Glass Onion Pictures

First published in Great Britain in 2003 by Hodder Wayland, an imprint of
Hodder Children's Books.

This paperback edition published in 2005

Reprinted in 2007 by Wayland, an imprint of Hachette Children's Books

British Library Cataloguing in Publication Data
Everett, Charles
   The Changing Face of Poland
   1. Poland - History - 1989 - Juvenile literature
   I. Title II. Everett, Barbara III. Poland
   943.8'057

ISBN 978 0 7502 4075 8

Printed and bound in China

Hachette Children's Books
338 Euston Road, London NW1 3BH

FIFE COUNCIL WEST AREA	
788811	
PETERS	14-Aug-07
J914.38	£6.99
JPEO	DP

Acknowledgements
The publishers would like to thank
the following for their contributions
to this book: Rob Bowden – statistics
research; Peter Bull – map illustration;
Nick Hawken – statistics panel
illustrations. All photographs are
by Jenny Matthews except: Impact
Photos 13; Popperfoto 11 & 43.

▲ This map shows the main geographical features of Poland, as well as places mentioned in this book.

POLAND: KEY FACTS

Area: 312,677 sq km

Population: 38.6 million

Population density: 124 people per sq km

Capital city: Warsaw

Other major cities: Cracow, Poznan, Wroclaw, Gdansk, Szczecin, Torun, Lodz, Bialystok, Rzeszow.

Highest mountain: Rysy (2,499 m).

Longest rivers: Vistula, Oder, Bug.

Main language: Polish

Major religion: Roman Catholicism

Currency: The zloty

2 Past Times

◀ *Auschwitz concentration camp was built during the German occupation in the Second World War. An estimated 1.5 million people died here between 1940 and 1945. Today, Auschwitz serves as a monument to this terrible time that did so much to shape the history of post-war Europe.*

Communist rule

After the Second World War, the Soviet Union (or USSR) took control of Poland and several other Eastern European countries that had been occupied by Nazi Germany. It forced them to form their own communist-style governments. Together, these countries became known as the 'Eastern Bloc'.

Under communism, the standard of living was generally much lower than in Western Europe and people had less freedom, too. This led to unrest throughout the Eastern bloc. In 1980 a wave of protests swept Poland. A free trades-union movement emerged called 'Solidarity', led by the dockyard worker Lech Walesa. Solidarity forced the government to make wide changes in civil rights. In December 1981, under pressure from the USSR, Solidarity was banned and Lech Walesa was imprisoned and many political and civil rights were suspended as the military ruled the country under martial law. However, during the following few years support for Solidarity continued to grow, while the government failed to solve the country's problems.

Transition: from Communism to capitalism

At the end of the 1980s, the whole world was taken by surprise as one by one the communist regimes of the Eastern bloc collapsed. Because the Solidarity movement was so strong, Poland was one of the first of the Eastern bloc countries to introduce reforms. Lech Walesa became the first freely elected president.

By 2000 Poland had become one of the most economically successful of the former Eastern bloc countries. However, there are things people miss about the old days. Although their freedom was restricted in many ways, communism in Poland was never as strict as in the USSR – for example, people were able to own property, go to church and travel abroad. Prices of goods and property were low and there were many things that the state used to provide cheaply or for free that people must pay for now.

▶ *The Palace of Culture in Warsaw was a gift from the Soviet Union to symbolize the friendship between the two countries.*

IN THEIR OWN WORDS

'My name is Anka Watrobska and I have worked for the Cracow Opera for twenty years. On the whole, life is better now. I have a passport – it used to be difficult to get one. I can say what I want and there is everything in the shops. But today we live with uncertainty. In the past your job was guaranteed but now the manager can suddenly decide to sack you. We don't even know if the Opera will continue to exist. There are big financial problems. In the past the seats were subsidized. Now, the cheapest seats are 25–30 zlotys, which is too much for ordinary people to pay.'

3 Landscape and Climate

The North European Plain

Stretching 6,500 km from the North Sea to the Ural Mountains, the North European Plain is like a natural corridor between Russia and Western Europe, and Poland is right in the middle of this region. Bounded to the north by the Baltic Sea and to the south by the Carpathian Mountains, most of Poland is low-lying and fertile. The retreat of the ice sheets at the end of the last ice age, 10,000 years ago, left thousands of beautiful lakes scattered across the landscape, particularly in the north.

Mountains

The hills and mountains of the Sudeten and Carpathian ranges stretch along the 950 km of Poland's southern border. With peaks of over 2,500 m, the Tatra mountains on the Slovak border are the highest mountains in Poland and look very similar to the Alps. Most of the mountains, however, are less steep and covered in forest.

▲ *Thousands of lakes like this one are scattered across the northern half of Poland and for many Poles they are a favourite destination for weekends and holidays.*

Forests

Twenty-nine per cent of Poland's land area is covered in forest (compared to around 10 per cent in Great Britain, for example). Polish forests include some of the oldest woodlands in Europe. In eastern Poland these forests are renowned for large wild animals such as bison, elk, bears and wolves, which disappeared from most other parts of Europe a long time ago.

▼ *The Vistula is the largest river in Poland, and flows from south to north through many of Poland's largest centres of population, including Cracow and Warsaw.*

Rivers

Three major rivers, the Oder, the Bug and the Vistula, flow from the uplands in the south to the Baltic Sea in the North. The largest and longest of these is the Vistula which flows 1,090 km from its source near the Slovak border, through Cracow and Warsaw, before reaching the Baltic Sea at Gdansk.

IN THEIR OWN WORDS

'I am Grzegorz Okolow and I am a forester and education officer at the Kampinoska National Park near Warsaw. I was born in the middle of the ancient forest of Bialwieza and my father was a forester too, which influenced me a lot in my choice of career. In the past the forest was seen as a wood factory – providing material for firewood and building. Now there is strong pressure for the forest to be a place for recreation and tourism. More Poles have their own transport these days and they want to get out of the towns and enjoy nature. However, it can be difficult to get the right balance between tourism and protecting the forest environment.'

A changing climate?

Poland is usually described as having a typical continental climate, with warm summers and cold winters, but there are signs that the climate may be changing. In recent years, the normal weather patterns have been rather disrupted. Summertime temperatures have been reaching record levels and winter temperatures have been very erratic. In December 2001, for example, Poland had some of the heaviest snows for thirty years and temperatures below –20 °C. Then, in January 2002, the temperatures suddenly soared to around 18 °C for a few days, which is much higher than normal for the time of year.

▲ *Contrary to what many foreigners believe, Poland enjoys a warm sunny climate for much of the year. Eating outside is popular during the summer months.*

▼ *There is evidence that the Polish climate is becoming more extreme, with heavier rainfall.*

Extreme weather

Severe storms have caused widespread damage to trees, buildings and power supplies. Flooding has also been a big problem. In July 1997, 140,000 people were evacuated from their homes because of flooding in the Oder and upper Vistula valleys. At the time this was seen as a freak event but there have been several serious floods since. These events may be partly the result of global climate change but human activities in the local environment also have an effect. Forest damage around the headwaters of the rivers Oder and Vistula and straightening of the river courses make flooding more severe as water runs off more quickly. Also, widespread building development on flood plains means that there is more damage when the floods come.

IN THEIR OWN WORDS

'My name is Dr Malgorzata Mierkiewicz. I am a
hydrologist working at the Institute of Meteorology.
It's difficult to say if weather patterns have changed.
There have always been floods and droughts. One
of the reasons why flooding is such a problem is
that people build houses and factories too close to
water. In 1997 there were catastrophic floods on
the Oder, with fifty-five people dying. A large area
near the river in Wroclow was flooded, but
afterwards people rebuilt in exactly the same area,
which is a flood plain. With help from the World
Bank, we now have a more modern meteorological
service and can give better and faster flood warnings.'

Flood defences in Poland have become a major priority for
both the government and the international community.
The International Monetary Fund has committed hundreds
of millions of dollars to restoring damaged infrastructure
and improving flood prevention schemes.

▼ *There have been several major floods like this over the last few years. It is uncertain
whether or not this is due to climate change, but changes in water management and
building development could go a long way to reducing the damage.*

4

Natural Resources

Energy sources

Most of Poland's electricity comes from burning its large reserves of coal. This is a cheap energy source but it causes a lot of pollution. The government is trying to reduce the amount of coal used by encouraging the building of new oil- and gas-burning power stations and opening up the power industry to private companies. Recent figures show that 73 per cent of Poland's electricity was generated by burning coal, compared with 77 per cent in 1990.

Only 1.5 per cent of Poland's power is generated from renewable energy sources, compared to an average of 6 per cent in each European Union (EU) country, but the government aims to increase their use. This has been strongly supported by the EU through aid programmes and 'debt for environment swaps'. Since 1991, a number of countries that are owed money by Poland have agreed to let Poland use some of the money for environmental improvements, instead of paying them back. The money is administered by the Polish Ecofund Foundation, which currently lists renewable energy as a top priority.

▼ *Power lines in the Carpathian Mountains near Bielsko-Biala carry electricity. Burning coal is still the main way to generate electricity, but the government is working to reduce Poland's dependence on coal.*

IN THEIR OWN WORDS

'I am Wojciech Rudzki, I'm a civil engineer and I live in Warsaw. There is a very cheap and efficient system for heating buildings here in the city. At power stations steam is produced as part of the process of generating electricity. Usually it is just allowed to escape into the air. But in Warsaw it goes into a network of pipes and is used to heat water for central heating. The pipes are buried deep underground so they are fine even when it's –20 °C and the earth is frozen.

'I know that people are investigating the use of alternative energy – wind energy on the coast and biomass energy in our lake district. There are also some geothermal and hydroelectric schemes, but really the energy system hasn't changed because it doesn't need to. We actually produce more electricity than we need and sell the extra to Austria and Germany.'

Minerals

As well as having resources of sulphur, natural gas, silver and lead, Poland is a major copper exporter. The Polish copper company, KGHM, based in Lublin, is the seventh-largest copper producer in the world. In 1991 KGHM was 100 per cent state owned and employed about 48,000 people. Today it is over half owned by private shareholders and has 18,000 employees. Many divisions of KGHM have become independent companies. They sell their services to KGHM, and employ a lot of the former KGHM workers.

Polish copper reserves are expected to last for another thirty years. KGHM has been branching out into areas like telecommunications and gas and electricity supplies to ensure its long-term survival and to help the local economy become less dependent on copper.

▼ *Traditionally mining has been important in Poland and today many Polish jobs rely on this industry. However, it is likely that Poland will be burning less coal in the future as mineral deposits will not last forever.*

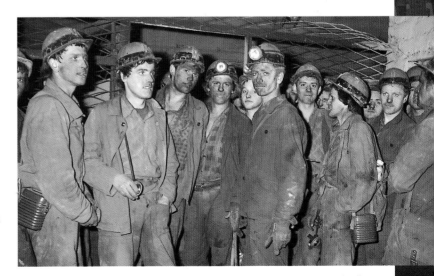

Agriculture

Sixty per cent of Poland's land area is used as farmland. Most farms are small and traditional farming methods are widespread. There are still a million horses working on Polish farms, and pesticides and fertilizers are used much less than in Western Europe.

During the communist period, Polish farmers were generally quite well off. In contrast to other Eastern Bloc countries, Polish farms were not taken over by the government and operated as large state-owned businesses. Instead, farms generally remained small and privately owned. The government guaranteed to buy their produce for a certain price and they could sell their produce privately too.

Now farmers have to compete with foreign imports and often have to find a way of earning extra income, for example by providing holiday accommodation or through a second job. Many have found that organic farming is a way to beat the competition from abroad – because of their traditional methods, many Polish farms are ideal for growing organic produce. The government passed the Organic Farming Act in 1991, to bring Polish standards into line with strict regulations in the European Union.

Agricultural workers
(% of total working population)

50
40 — 39 (1970)
30 — 29 (1980)
26 (1995)
20
10
0
1970   1980   1995

Source: Geographical Digest

▲ The number of agricultural workers in Poland as a percentage of the working population is declining.

◀ Whereas in Western Europe farming has become highly mechanized, scenes like this of a family haymaking are still commonplace in the Polish countryside.

Forestry

Only a small part of the Polish economy is directly based on forestry but Polish forests are some of the richest ecosystems in Europe. The state owns about three-quarters of the 28 million hectares of forest in Poland. Industrial pollution and neglect have caused serious problems in some areas but since the early 1990s, with support from the international community, the State Forest Enterprise has made wide-ranging improvements. A national forest plan was adopted by the government in 1995 which aims to increase Poland's forest cover to 30 per cent by the year 2020.

▲ *This farmer is gathering his crop of beetroots by hand. Small-scale agriculture like this makes little use of artificial fertilizers and pesticides but has difficulty competing with large-scale farming abroad.*

IN THEIR OWN WORDS

'My name is Irena Fraszczak and I run an organic farm near Porabka, in the Beskid Maly Mountains. There used to be a lot of small farms here in the mountains but now it's very hard to make a living from them. We have 1.5 hectares of farmland, with 0.7 hectares of forest. We started offering holiday accommodation two years ago. Most of our guests are Polish but we also get some Dutch and German visitors. I run the farm and the holiday business and I also have four children to look after. My husband Ryszard has a job in town.'

5

The Changing Environment

Urbanization

The percentage of Poles living in cities has been increasing ever since the Second World War. During the communist period, when urbanization was part of government policy, the population of Cracow tripled in thirty years. Workers in the new state industries moved into the high-rise housing that sprang up around the cities. Today, suburban areas are growing as people move out of the tower blocks into new houses.

Traffic

In the 1980s fewer people had cars, fuel was rationed and everybody used public transport. During the 1990s the traffic on Polish roads roughly doubled and it is expected to double again by 2015. To cope with this, the government is undertaking a major programme of road and motorway building that will bring Poland's infrastructure up to European Union standards.

▶ *Tower blocks like these are a legacy of communist housing policy. A lot more people can afford to buy or build houses now but there are still many people living in these neighbourhoods.*

IN THEIR OWN WORDS

'I am Marcin Hyla, I'm from Cracow and I'm a bicycle activist! Transport is a pretty big problem, one of the most important features of the changes that are affecting Poland in fact. Before 1989 car use was very limited. Cars were very expensive and petrol was not always available – you needed coupons to buy it. Most people travelled by public transport.

'From the beginning of the 1990s people started buying cars and there was a 40 per cent growth in new car sales for several consecutive years. Since 1987 there have been protests by cyclists, with a symbolic 'no car' day once a year. Until the 1990s street actions by cyclists had a low profile, but then they became more organized, getting press coverage and using T-shirts and posters as publicity.'

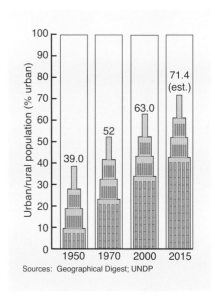

The road system needs modernizing but environmental groups are concerned that, as in the West, traffic will just increase to fill whatever road capacity there is. They want a transport policy that encourages people to use other forms of transport, such as railways, trams and bikes, as much as possible. In Gdansk, for example, a project is being funded by the international community to provide 100 km of cycleways. Road vehicles are a major source of greenhouse gases and the increase in traffic may make it hard for Poland to fulfil international agreements on reducing carbon dioxide emissions.

Sources: Geographical Digest; UNDP

▼ *Major new road building projects are changing the Polish landscape. Improving the infrastructure is vital to enable Poland's economy to develop, but the more roads that are built, the more cars there will be and the more pollution.*

▲ *The number of people living in cities as a proportion of the total population is rising, and will continue to do so.*

Pollution

During the 1980s Poland was among the most polluted countries in Europe. Heavy industry, coal-fired power stations and a lack of waste-water treatment all contributed to the problem but the situation has improved a lot. Environmental activists have played an important role in publicising the pollution problems. As well as passing laws and giving incentives to businesses to improve the environment, the government has greatly increased the amount of money it spends on pollution control. Poland has adopted the European Union's Integrated Pollution Prevention Directive and has signed international agreements on a wide range of environmental issues.

◄ *A coal-fired power station in Gdansk. Although many of the heavily polluting iron and steel foundries in the south have closed, Poland is still one of Europe's largest consumers of coal.*

There is less air pollution now because many industrial plants have shut down whilst others have become cleaner. But the amount of coal being burned to generate electricity is still a problem. Burning coal releases sulphur dioxide, which is dissolved by water in the atmosphere and falls as acid rain. This kills trees and the wildlife in lakes and rivers, as well as damaging buildings. There is also a lot more traffic now than there used to be and this is a new threat to air quality, especially in urban areas.

The decline in heavy industry has reduced water pollution and river pollution has dropped by 50 per cent. However, there are still problems with untreated waste water from large urban areas. The National Environmental Policy has given the construction of waste-water treatment plants top priority.

▲ *These days the Polish streets are full of foreign cars. During the 1980s, if people owned cars at all they were usually models produced in Poland or the Soviet Union.*

IN THEIR OWN WORDS

'I am Dr Konstany Radziwill. I'm a family doctor and I'm also chair of the Polish Family Doctors' Organization. Health has improved a lot since the early 1990s because of environmental changes. Heavy industry caused such a lot of pollution. The aluminium smelters and steel mills contaminated the water. The mines used water for processing ore and the minerals washed into the rivers and poisoned them. This is what happened to the Vistula – it was almost dead, but now it has returned to life with more fish.

'Some people are not happy that the mines and factories have closed because they have lost their jobs, but the air and water are less polluted so everyone else benefits.'

The 'throw away' society

Many goods were difficult to get or rationed in the 1980s, so people did not throw much away. If things could be re-used they generally were. This did not apply just to the goods themselves but to the packaging too. People used to keep plastic shopping bags rather than throw them away and all kinds of containers were recycled.

Nowadays most goods are sold in disposable containers and bags. It is often easier and cheaper to buy new appliances than to fix old ones. Poland faces the same problems with municipal waste as the USA and Western Europe. Local authorities across the country are setting up recycling schemes and a big effort is being made to increase public awareness. The 'Clean Up Poland' campaign started in 1994. Since then it has been working with the media, schools, town councils and businesses to highlight the problem and to put pressure on the authorities to take action.

▲ On average people produce over 300 kg of waste per head a year in Poland. At present most of this is being buried, but there is increasing pressure to increase recycling.

◄ There is a growing awareness in Poland of the need to find ways of dealing with the ever-increasing amount of waste. Although recycling was common in communist days, it never needed to deal with the sheer volume and variety of rubbish generated by Polish consumers today.

Mountains of scrap

Between 1994 and 1998 the number of cars sold in Poland increased from 266,000 to 644,000, and there could be as many as 15 million cars in Poland by 2010. During the 1990s there were few facilities for recycling the materials from scrap cars, although tyres have been used as fuel in industrial furnaces. Now a junk vehicle recycling programme is underway that will establish a nationwide network of environmentally friendly scrapyards. The government has also banned the import of damaged cars, thousands of which were being imported into Poland to be repaired and sold.

▲ *These workers have a full-time job sorting waste at a recycling centre in Warsaw.*

IN THEIR OWN WORDS

'My name is Mira Stanislawska-Meysztowicz and I am Chair of the 'Clean Up Poland' campaign. We try to teach a new approach to the environment and to raise ecological awareness. I work with a lot of schoolchildren. In a village near Warsaw there was illegal dumping in a stream. Schoolchildren asked their parents to help clean it up. They put some benches there and now have a nice place to eat their lunch. However, our campaign isn't just about picking up rubbish – it's about changing the way people think, to reduce the amount of waste we produce in the first place. For instance, we are trying to get people to choose goods with less packaging, or at least packaging that can be recycled.'

6

The Changing Population

Longer life expectancy

Life expectancy has improved in Poland since the early 1980s and this may be partly due to a better environment in large urban areas. In 1980 people were living 70.1 years on average but by 1998 this figure had gone up to 73 years. Infant mortality has decreased too; it went down from over 19 per 1,000 in 1990, to 9 per 1,000 in 1998.

Shrinking population

Although fewer children are dying and people are living longer, the population growth rate in Poland slowed dramatically during the 1990s. The first decline in the post-war period was seen in 1999 when the population dropped by about 13,000. What is happening to the Polish population reflects global trends towards a slowing down of population increase. As they become more developed many countries experience population decline for a number of reasons. Poland, for example, has become a land of opportunity and young people often feel there is more to life than starting a family. The birth rate has decreased despite new laws restricting access to birth control. Abortion is now only permitted on medical grounds or when pregnancy is the result of a criminal act, whilst contraceptives are expensive and generally not available on prescription.

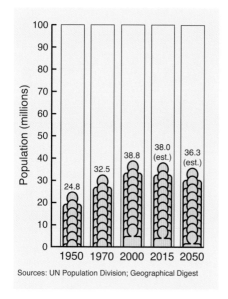

Sources: UN Population Division; Geographical Digest

▲ *These figures show that Poland's population is expected to fall by around 2.5 million by 2050.*

▶ *Young couples like this are less likely than their parents to start a family. Many young couples in Poland are dedicating their lives to work and leisure and having children is less of a priority.*

Ageing population

The estimated number of births for 1999 was 382,000 compared to 723,000 in 1983. The combination of low birth rates and longer life expectancy means that the average age of the population as a whole is increasing. Forecasts predict that the number of pensioners will outnumber workers by 2025. If this happens then the next generation of Polish workers will need to pay high taxes to support their parent's generation.

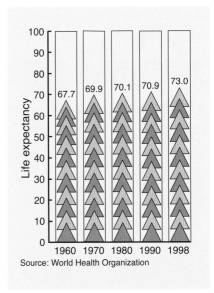

Source: World Health Organization

▲ Polish people can expect to live five years longer than forty years previously.

◀ These elderly musicians have a longer life expectancy than the previous generation. This is largely due to better diet and improved healthcare.

IN THEIR OWN WORDS

'Hi, I'm Patrycja Matuszewska, I live in Warsaw and I work as a freelance writer for *Marie Claire* magazine, as well as writing film scripts. I'd like to get a job in television.

'A lot of my friends, people who are in their early twenties, are TV producers or have jobs in the media. Young people here are a lot more self-confident today and they have higher expectations of what life can offer. I have a rented apartment, a car and enough money to live on, although I can't afford the sort of lifestyle advertisers like to show us! I hope to have children one day, but I'm in no hurry!'

The Polish people

The percentage of Polish citizens belonging to ethnic and racial minorities is one of the lowest in Europe. In 1999 it was estimated that, of the Polish population, 97.6 per cent were Poles, with Germans, Ukrainians, Roma and Byelorussians making up most of the rest. However, although their numbers are still comparatively small, there are more non-European residents than before, particularly from countries in the former Soviet Union.

◄ Roma musicians entertain the public in Cracow's streets. The influence of immigrant communities has done much to enrich Polish culture over the centuries.

Immigration

Poland had very few immigrants under communism but since the reforms of 1989 foreigners have been attracted by the opportunities there. People of many nationalities have arrived with foreign companies, or in search of business opportunities, but the biggest immigration is from the east and also from the Balkan countries to the south, especially from the Roma population. To the people of the poorer countries of the former Soviet Union Poland promises an easier life. Economic migrants and refugees are attracted to Poland in the same way that Poles were attracted to Western Europe in the 1980s.

Poland has little experience of racial diversity. The Second World War and the closed communist government that followed ended Poland's position at the crossroads of Europe with its vibrant ethnic mix. Many young people do not learn very much about the Holocaust in the Second World War that systematically murdered Jews, Roma people and others, often in concentration camps located, like Auschwitz, in Poland. At the moment there is a lack of public awareness of the problems of racism. It is likely that many more immigrants from the East will arrive in Poland over the next few decades and Polish people will have to adapt, once again, to a more cosmopolitan society.

▲ *Many of the traders at this large market have come from abroad to sell their goods. To her neighbours in the East, Poland is a land of plenty.*

IN THEIR OWN WORDS

'Hi, my name is Sherin Helmy and I'm 18. My father is Egyptian and my mother is Polish. Unfortunately Poland is not multicultural and I've never met another Muslim girl my age, but no one is unkind or intolerant. I don't exactly feel like the odd one out but I do feel different; it's rare to see a non-white face. A lot of Romanians, Russians and Ukrainians come here to do low-paid jobs, and Koreans and Chinese bring cheap products such as shirts to sell in the markets. It's a problem because the foreigners work or sell their goods for less than Polish people do. Many old people find it difficult to accept foreigners but it doesn't matter so much to young people.'

Distribution of wealth

In the communist period the government kept prices low and provided everyone with jobs and homes. Skilled professionals earned the same wages as unskilled workers and there were limited opportunities for getting rich. Now skilled people can get well-paid jobs but everybody must find work for themselves.

Since the reforms of the 1990s incomes have risen significantly and the growing middle class enjoys a standard of living comparable to that in Western Europe. However, many Poles, especially of the older generation and people in rural areas, feel they are still waiting to see any benefit from the changes that have taken place. The basic cost of living is far higher than it used to be and, for many people, wages have not kept up. Alongside the new Polish middle class there are groups, particularly in rural areas, that suffer from long-term poverty.

▲ *Designer labels are readily available to shoppers in many cities in Poland – if they can afford them.*

◀ *Among the new generation of Poles there are plenty who can afford smart new houses, like these in the wealthy suburb of Isabellin in Warsaw.*

IN THEIR OWN WORDS

'I'm Samanta Bednarska and I'm 21. I'm a second-year student at Gdansk Polytechnic. I have a small fifth-floor flat in the old town, but unfortunately to pay for it I have to work from 4 p.m. till midnight in a convenience store. It's been a good experience for me to find out what the real world is like, but I'm not sure I'll be able to carry on both working and studying. I have a great boyfriend and he's very supportive but I have no plans to get married yet – I want to travel and find out more about the world for myself.'

Family life

Because of a constant housing shortage during the communist years, it was common for parents, grandparents and children to share a small flat. The extended family is still an important feature of Polish life. Grandparents often play a big part in bringing up children. Young people often live with their parents until they get married, even though it has become easier for them to be financially independent.

▲ *During the communist period, young people had to wait years to get a flat in a block like this and, often, young couples had to live with their parents. Today there are still many people living in blocks of flats, but there is a wider choice of accommodation for those who can afford their own houses.*

Most couples do get married but attitudes are changing. It is becoming less unusual for couples to live together without getting married. The average age at which people get married is rising, as people often choose to concentrate on their careers first. The divorce rate is also rising and with the increase in the number of single-parent families there is a small but noticeable trend away from traditional family life.

Women's roles

In Poland there is a widely held view that a woman's place is in the home and that mothers are responsible for passing on Polish culture to the next generation. Communist ideology includes the idea that men and women are equal and the communist government encouraged women to go out to work, but even during that period traditional Polish attitudes never really changed: men never shared women's traditional work in the home.

A national action plan for women containing a list of objectives designed to improve women's equality was supposed to take effect in 2001 but has been delayed. At the beginning of the 1990s there was a backlash against communism and a trend for women to return to traditional roles. During the last decade of reforms, women's rights have not been seen as a priority and laws protecting them have been weakened. The Catholic Church, which has a lot of influence on the government, promotes traditional roles for women.

▲ *A mother pushes her child on a swing while her husband is at work. Generally, women in Poland play a traditional role in the family. It is unusual for men to be in charge of childcare and housework.*

Religion

Ninety per cent of Poles are Roman Catholic. During the communist years the Catholic Church often criticized the government. When the Polish Cardinal Joseph Wojtyla became Pope John Paul II in 1978, the Church became a rallying point in the fight for freedom and democracy. There was widespread discontent with the government and practically everyone went to church.

IN THEIR OWN WORDS

'My name is Barbara Adamus. I am a deacon in the Protestant Church. Since 1985 I have taught religion to Protestant children in schools. When I was at school there was only myself and one other girl who were Protestants and we had a difficult time because we didn't join in the Catholic religious ceremonies.

'Some years ago when I was living in a small community my congregation wanted me to become their pastor but it wasn't possible at the time. In theory there is nothing to stop me being a pastor now but many of my male colleagues are against the idea.'

High church attendance continued into the nineties and today the number of practising Catholics in Poland is still one of the highest in the world. Nonetheless, not everyone is happy about the Church's power and the political part it plays in Polish life. A growing number of Poles are turning to other, non-Catholic, denominations, in search of a simpler approach to God.

◀ *A typical Sunday scene at a Polish church. Services are always well attended. Most people go to church occasionally and many go regularly.*

Education

The education system has been undergoing big changes since 1999. Also, there was no system for monitoring the many new private schools. Polish school qualifications are being brought into line with the rest of Europe in preparation for Poland joining the EU, so an effective system for monitoring all schools is needed.

The reforms also aim to address regional inequalities. Many schools in the countryside are still educating their pupils as if they were going to be guaranteed jobs in the state factories. Generally, people value education today more than in the past because they see it as the way to get a good job and a better standard of living, but in the countryside people's expectations are lower. Although most students have to pay to go to university now, the number of university graduates has tripled since the beginning of the 1990s. However, school leavers in rural areas are much less likely to go on to higher education.

▼ *Piotr Gatlik, front right, and his fellow students are hoping that their education will provide them with the opportunity to have a good career and a high standard of living.*

IN THEIR OWN WORDS

'My name is Mariola Mikoiajczyk. I am head of a primary school in Myslenice, a small town near Cracow. We have 600 pupils aged 7–12, and our school day starts at 8 a.m. and finishes at 3 p.m.

'I was a headteacher under communist rule and I've seen quite a few changes since communism came to an end. Religion and Information Technology have been added to the curriculum, and children usually study English or German now instead of Russian. Schools have less money and get less support from the government. In the past there were extra classes for hobbies such as photography, but now parents have to pay for these.'

Healthcare and medicine

The health service has a lot of problems but major changes are taking place. Under communism it was run by central government but it did not have enough money to work properly and was very inefficient. During the 1990s, a special tax was introduced to pay for healthcare. Regional health authorities were set up to buy services from both state and private healthcare providers. However, many health authorities are short of money and hospitals have run up large debts. As well as having to pay for medicines prescribed by their doctors, patients often find they have to pay extra for treatment and people often cannot afford the healthcare they need. Despite these problems, campaigns to raise awareness about health issues, like diet and smoking, have led to significant improvements in public health.

▼ *These children are enjoying a salt spray tonic at a health spa.*

Diet

There has been a dramatic decline in heart disease in Poland since the early 1990s and this is probably mainly due to changes in the Polish diet. During communist times, meat was subsidized and the supply of fresh fruit and vegetables was mainly limited to what Poland could produce itself. At the beginning of the 1990s subsidies for meat were replaced with taxes, making meat and products based on animal fats more expensive. There was a lot of

publicity about healthy eating and the importance of a low-fat diet. At the same time, Poland began to import a lot more fresh fruit and vegetables.

Poland has a strong tradition of meat eating, and in the past, vegetarianism was regarded as very strange. Now vegetarianism is more acceptable. At the beginning of the 1990s it was almost impossible to get a vegetarian meal at a hotel or restaurant, but now vegetarian food is not hard to find.

▲ In the communist days, people could get cheap meals in restaurants serving traditional Polish dishes but now these have gone. Today, Western-style fast food like hamburgers and pizza are taken for granted by the younger generation.

◀ Home-grown fresh fruit and vegetables are still available in markets in Poland, but much food has now to be imported.

Shopping

During the 1980s many goods were rationed and people had to queue even for everyday necessities. Many luxuries and Western imports were only available in special dollar shops. In fact, the US dollar was like an unofficial currency. However, Poles were usually not able to change their money legally and a dollar from an illegal moneychanger cost about half a day's wages.

Since the reforms of the 1990s both the quantity and variety of goods available in the shops has increased enormously and the zloty has much greater value. Shopping in Poland now is much like shopping in any other European country. There are hypermarkets and shopping malls with outlets for all the internationally well-known brands.

▲ *Today, as in the West, advertising is everywhere. Advertisements like this one for a supermarket on the side of a bus are a very obvious sign of how times have changed.*

IN THEIR OWN WORDS

'I am Halina Augustyniak and I'm 74. Shopping is completely different now from the way it used to be. There used to be queues for everything. Once I had to queue nine hours for some butter. Now the shops are full and there are advertisements everywhere encouraging people to buy. But as more big shops are built, the small shops are forced to close because they can't cope with the competition. In the supermarket everything looks good but you often get rubbish inside the packaging.'

Leisure

A generation ago, leisure activities ranging from holiday camps to sports clubs, arts and entertainment were organized by the state or by the state enterprises. Big subsidies made these activities available to all because the communists saw leisure as a worker's right as well as an opportunity to educate people.

Now people see their leisure time as an opportunity to follow their own interests, instead of being directed by the state into certain activities. The choices are much wider and the leisure industry has become big business. More people have their own transport, which has opened up new opportunities to travel within Poland and across Europe, and many more people take holidays abroad. New 'extreme' sports, such as snowboarding and paragliding, which have captured the imaginations of young people around the world, are popular in Poland too.

▲ *The smart new Frederick Chopin airport in Warsaw was built during the 1990s. In the past it was difficult to travel abroad but now foreign holidays are very popular.*

▼ *Although not so many people are online as in the West, the numbers are growing. Young people in Poland use computers and the Internet for playing, socializing and entertainment as much as for work.*

Music, film and fashion

During communist times Polish music and films dominated radio stations and cinemas. Now most cinemas show American films and the radio stations play a lot of American and British music. There is a broadcasting law that requires stations to broadcast Polish programmes for a minimum of 30 per cent of the time but many artists choose to sing in English. Some people are

IN THEIR OWN WORDS

'Hi! My name is Michael Markiewicz, I'm 23 and music is my life. I play the double bass and the piano, but in our band, Diktum, I'm the singer. Our music is modern rock, not very popular in Poland where pop music is the only thing people listen to. We all have different day jobs – I work in a photo agency, for example – but we really want to be full-time musicians. We write our own songs – in English. Our dream is to play abroad where we think we would be more appreciated.'

concerned that Poland is losing its national identity but the influence of Western culture seems here to stay.

In the 1980s, young Poles tended to be a little behind Western fashions and a visitor from the West might have noticed a difference in how people looked on the street. Now Poles have access to all the well-known brands and young city people in Poland look just as trendy as anywhere else.

▼ *Breakdancing is just one of the many activities that the young people of Poland enjoy doing – or just watching.*

8 Changes at Work

In communist times people used to joke, 'We pretend to work and the government pretends to pay us.' Large state-owned industries such as ship building, iron- and steel-making, and mining provided millions of jobs and there was little unemployment. However, these industries were often inefficient, or they produced more than was actually needed. They relied on large subsidies from the government and guaranteed buyers for their products. When the Eastern bloc collapsed at the end of the 1980s, industries had to become profitable or close down. Many factories closed and between 1990 and 1993 the unemployment rate rose from 6.3 per cent to 16.4 per cent.

Privatization

Between 1990 and 1999, 72 per cent of Polish industries were partly or wholly privatized. Sometimes privatization involved the managers or employees of a company buying the company's assets (such as buildings and equipment), and then running the company themselves. In other cases shares were offered for sale to foreign investors or investment bonds to the general public. Many large companies have become partly privatized with the government keeping a large share.

▲ The GNP per capita more than doubled from 1985 to 2000.

Source: World Bank; Data for 1975 not available

◄ The Nowa Huta steelworks in Cracow laid off much of its workforce in the early 1990s when it underwent restructuring. Despite the changes of the 1990s, the Polish steel industry still receives subsidies from the government.

◀ *Solidarity was born here, in the shipyards of Gdansk. Today the Polish shipbuilding industry still manages to compete with its global competitors although its long-term future is uncertain.*

Privatization was relatively easy in industries that were not heavily subsidized. However, by the end of the 1990s, privatization in heavy industries like iron and steel had hardly begun. The subsidies that the government pays to these industries are an obstacle to Poland joining the European Union, because they give Polish industry an advantage over non-subsidized competitors in other countries.

IN THEIR OWN WORDS

'I am Marian Formela and I work in the shipyard at Gdansk. It's a great feeling to work on a ship and see it launched. This shipyard is pretty old-fashioned, the equipment is ancient, and we don't know how long it will keep going. Still, there aren't many other shipyards in Western Europe now so the orders do keep coming to us and it is cheap to build a ship in Gdansk. At the moment we are working on a 45,000 tonne container ship for a German owner and when this is finished we have orders for two more.'

Private companies and foreign investment

Even during the 1970s, under communist rule private businesses made up about 10 per cent of the country's economy. By the year 2000, Poland had 2 million registered businesses (about one for every 19 Poles) and there was a record 13 billion dollars of foreign investment. Today, private and foreign businesses make up 79 per cent of the country's economic activity.

The arrival of foreign businesses in Poland has had good and bad effects. In many cases foreign money has paid for much-

◀ The headquarters of the Amplico AIG Life building in Gdansk. This is typical of the kind of new, foreign business that brings jobs and money into Poland but also provides competition with local businesses.

needed modern equipment and for training to update people's skills. On the other hand, the arrival of new competition from abroad has sometimes put local industry under a lot of pressure. The retail industry and farming have been particularly hard hit. Owners of small businesses find it difficult to compete with the new supermarkets and international chain stores.

New industries and technologies

Information technology has been developing quickly since the early 1990s, although Poland still has some way to go before it catches up with Western Europe. A major limitation at the moment is the old-fashioned telecommunications system, which does not yet have the capacity to support Internet use on the same scale as in France, Germany or the UK, for example. However, Internet use is growing. In 2002 there were an estimated 3 million computers with Internet access and this figure is increasing by about 30 per cent a year.

Service industries such as banking and insurance were very underdeveloped under communism and Poland has had to set up economic systems to allow these industries to develop. This has made the need for information technology even greater.

▲ *The banking industry and financial services have been built almost from scratch since the end of communism. Where there are cash points now, there were only black market dollar dealers in the 1980s.*

IN THEIR OWN WORDS

'My name is Tomasz Turzyriski and I am studying computer science. Computers are my life – my parents gave me my first one when I was 14 and I've been working with them ever since. You'll find most people working in computers here in Poland are young – in their twenties. It's good that more people are using computers and the Internet, although it's still a small percentage, and mostly in the cities. Many people in my neighbourhood have the Internet at home thanks to a local area network (LAN) project. If people aren't connected to this, the Internet is very expensive because there is only one phone company in Poland and it has the monopoly.'

Job security

During the communist period people could be almost certain of having a job throughout their working lives. But today there is much less job security in Poland, especially for older people. The number of jobs available depends on the success or failure of private businesses. These in turn are affected by changes in the world economy.

Between 1994 and 1998 there was a big drop in unemployment as the Polish economy was doing well, although this had little effect on the long-term unemployed. The financial crisis in Russia in 1998 had an impact on Polish jobs, many of which still rely on exports to Russia. Following this, the slowdown in the EU's economy had a bad effect on Polish exports, which brought further unemployment. By 2002 unemployment in Poland had reached its highest level since the early 1990s.

▲ *These men are getting together to discuss their experiences of being out of work. Despite the economic successes of the 1990s, unemployment is a problem which still affects the lives of a lot of people in Poland and it seems unlikely that it will go away.*

Women at work

During the 1970s and 1980s half the workforce was female. Although few were in politics or the top positions in companies, women were encouraged to work and study alongside men. The state provided a lot of support for working women with children, such as crèches and long maternity leave.

Since the end of communism there have been more women in top positions. For example, in 1992 Poland elected its first woman Prime Minister, Hanna Suchocka.

◀ *Selling pretzels from a street stall. A large proportion of people in low-paid jobs like this are women.*

Despite this, work has become more difficult for women in various ways. The huge job losses that have taken place as factories and industries have closed have tended to affect more women than men and the laws protecting women's rights in the workplace have been weakened. In the absence of state run crèches, working mothers must often look to the extended family for support.

IN THEIR OWN WORDS

'I am Barbara Mros, a mother of three (Alexandra, 10, Jeremy, 7, and Stansilas, 3). I'm in charge of personnel recruitment for a French consulting company. One noticeable change between my life and my mother's is working hours – in the past, women worked from 7 or 8 a.m. till 3 p.m., so by 4 p.m. my mother was always at home. Now we work the same hours as people in the West, 9 a.m. till 6 p.m. My parents and parents-in-law help a lot with the children after school but for families who don't have that support or who have to pay a childminder it's much more difficult, especially for the children.'

Tourism

Back in the 1980s, tourism was not well developed in Poland. Visitors from Western Europe needed visas to enter the country and had to supply the addresses where they would be staying during their visit. Although local prices were cheap, tourists had to change a minimum amount of money per day at the very low official exchange rate and hotels for foreigners were few and expensive.

Restrictions on foreign visitors were eased at the beginning of the 1990s. Since then the facilities for tourism have improved a lot. Throughout the 1990s, the number of tourists was on the increase and by the end of the decade Poland was high in the lists of popular tourist destinations in the world.

History and culture

Many tourists are attracted by Poland's rich history and culture. Poland has a tradition of staging international sporting and cultural events such as the Warsaw Autumn Festival and the annual international music festival at Sopot, near Gdansk. In the year 2000, Cracow held the title of European City of Culture.

▼ *Traditional Polish culture and folklore form an important part of the national identity and still play their part in contemporary life.*

Winter sports

The mountainous southern border of Poland has long been recognized as a great area for skiing but, until recently, the facilities on offer were quite limited. Now, however, there are many ski lifts and maintained pistes of all grades of difficulty, and Poland offers skiing enthusiasts a cheap alternative to the Alps.

Ecotourism

With the significant environmental improvements that have been made, Poland has begun to lose its bad reputation for pollution. Tourists are beginning to discover the rich variety of its wildlife and its natural beauty. A relatively new phenomenon, which is growing fast in Poland, is 'agrotourism'. Farms offer tourists accommodation, fresh produce and activities. Farm holidays are a new activity that takes advantage of Poland's unspoilt countryside.

▲ *With Poland's snowy winters, sports like skiing have always been popular. Nowadays, there are far more ski resorts than before.*

IN THEIR OWN WORDS

'My name is Kees Van Garderen and I run a small hotel with my wife Gerda in southern Poland. We are from the Netherlands and we came here after I lost my job. Running a guest house involves coping with a mass of regulations – a mix of those left over from the old times and their bureaucracy and the new ones brought in to prepare for EU membership. Tourism is still not very developed in Poland. If you go somewhere and ask for a leaflet, for example, it's rare for anything to be available. In my opinion, tourism is not such big business that it spoils the landscape with new building developments.'

9 The Way Ahead

Poland's peaceful transition from communism to democratic government and an economy based on private businesses is one of the most remarkable success stories of the 1990s. Other countries in similar situations are able to benefit from the Polish experience. Poland joined NATO in 1991 and has become an important member of the world community, taking a very active role in the United Nations. As well as participating in international aid programmes and peacekeeping initiatives, Poland is setting an example to the rest of the world in tackling environmental problems.

Poland has made many reforms to bring itself into line with other members of the European Union. One of the big challenges it still has to tackle is to find a way to reduce unemployment. Joining the European Union means that the government has to encourage privatization and remove the subsidies it pays to some industries, but this often leads to

▲ *A memorial to the Solidarity movement. Solidarity had a vital role in creating a free Poland and setting the scene for Poland to play an important role in modern Europe.*

◄ *There was a time not so long ago when jazz was banned in Poland because of its Western associations. Today's generation enjoys the freedom of expression that people in the West have always taken for granted.*

IN THEIR OWN WORDS

'Hi, I'm Aneta Jekot, I'm 18 and I'm a high school student. I have all sorts of opportunities that my parents did not have – I can learn English or French, for example, whereas my parents could learn only Russian. I can go on holiday to Spain, Italy or the UK but in the past it wasn't so easy. Next year I hope to go to university to study politics or something related to Europe. Poland is in the centre of Europe, but we are still seen as belonging to the East. Perhaps that impression will change when we are part of the European Union.'

more people losing their jobs. As the twenty-first century began the level of unemployment in Poland was rising instead of falling. Despite this, Poland is in a strong position to become a EU member and there is a strong desire in the EU to include Poland.

◀ *A new vision of the future? The architectural style of this new water sports centre in Gdansk is very different from the concrete of the communist era. It expresses the optimism of the Polish people and their hopes for the twenty-first century.*

Glossary

Capitalism The economic system in which individuals can make money increase (or decrease) through investment.

Communism A political system in which businesses are run by the state on behalf of the people and personal freedom is restricted. The Communist Party runs the country and although elections may be held all the candidates are from the same party.

Democracy A political system in which people choose the leaders they want to run the country by voting for them in elections.

Drought A long period with little or no rain.

Ecosystem A habitat; living things in their natural environment.

Emissions Waste gases or liquids produced by industry or transport.

European Union The group of countries in Europe united by certain common laws and, for many, a common currency, the euro.

Exports Goods that are sold to other countries.

Geothermal energy Energy from the internal heat of the earth.

GNP per capita GNP is Gross National Product, the amount of money that Poland earns from all the goods and services it produces. 'Per capita' means 'per person', so GNP per capita is the total earned divided by the total population.

Greenhouse gases Gases which cause the earth to heat up as if it was inside a greenhouse.

Heavy industry Industries such as coal-mining, shipbuilding and steel production.

Hydroelectricity Electricity generated by turbines that are turned by the force of falling water.

Hydrologist Someone who studies the location and movement of water.

Immigrants People who have left their home country and come to live in another.

Imports Goods that are bought from other countries.

Infant mortality The number of deaths of children aged under one year; it is usually measured as the number of deaths per 1,000 children that are born.

Infrastructure The network of transport links, communication links and power supplies that a country needs to have in order for its economy to work well.

International Monetary Fund An international organization set up after the Second World War to try to ensure worldwide economic stability. It lends money to governments.

Investment Something into which money is put with the hope of it increasing in value.

Life expectancy The average length of time that a person can expect to live.

Meteorology The study of the Earth's atmosphere, especially in relation to weather forecasting.

Municipal Relating to towns and cities.

NATO North Atlantic Treaty Organization, a military alliance between some countries in Western Europe and the USA, set up after the Second World War as a defence against the danger presented by the Soviet Union.

Rationing Limiting something, normally food, to a small amount.

Shares Parts of a company that you can own. If you own shares in a company you are a shareholder.

Subsidized Given money to help cover the cost of producing goods or providing services.

Trades union Workers form and join trades unions so that their interests can be represented.

United Nations An organization set up after the Second World War to promote international peace and co-operation.

Urbanization The process of an area becoming less rural; countryside turning into urban (city) areas.

USSR United Soviet Socialist Republics: the communist empire, also known as the Soviet Union.

Further Information

Books to read

Auschwitz by Clive Lawton (Watts, 2002)

Questioning History: The Cold War by
Sean Sheehan (Hodder Wayland, 2003)

Books for older readers

Lonely Planet Guide to Poland by Krzyssztof
Dydynski (Lonely Planet, 2002)

Poland by James A Michener (Fawcett
Books, 1990)

Useful address
Polish National Tourist Office in London
Level 3, Westec House
West Gate
London
W5 1YY
Tel: (+44) 8700 675 010
Fax: (+44) 8700 675 011

Index

Numbers in **bold** are pages where there is a photograph or illustration.